how to parent
Like An Autistic

K. BRON JOHNSON

Edited by: Andrea Zanin

Cover Art by: Angela Weddle

https://angela-weddle.pixels.com/

Title: How to Parent Like an Autistic

This publication has been assigned:

ISBN: 978-0-9780305-5-1

Large Print Edition

TABLE OF CONTENTS

How to Parent Like an Autistic

FOREWORD

By Nancy Getty, Author
https://www.aspergerrus.com/

Nobody knows what autism is. History has shown that autistic individuals have been both celebrated and chastised by society, yet the mysteries of autism remain unclear. Each autistic person is an individual who requires to be seen as a whole so they can be guided in their unique struggles and strengths to find a place of acceptance and comfort within their environment. To know they are safe and appreciated as a person.

Kelly Bron Johnson has laid out an honest guideline to assist parents and family members who share their lives with an autistic individual. This book will be highly useful for families that are seeking a path of discovery and acceptance in order to achieve a balance within the family unit. Kelly touches on areas of importance within the autistic person's life from a first-person autistic perspective that will allow you to see and experience a viewpoint that may seem foreign, but is real for the autistic person.

INTRODUCTION

In recent years, we've seen more and more women diagnosed with autism after their children receive a diagnosis. This was the case for me. In the last ten years or so, science has discovered that some autistic traits (sometimes understood as the broader autism phenotype) appear to run in families. Other times, autism seems to come out of the blue for a family. I find the latter families struggle the most, so this is who I have set out to help with this book.

My generation, meaning people born in the 1970s and 1980s, grew up in a system that didn't have a good understanding of autism. It was seen as a "male disorder," so many girls and women did not receive our autism diagnosis until adulthood. In plenty of cases, mine included, we only came to this revelation after one of our children was diagnosed. I received my official autism diagnosis almost two years after my son was diagnosed. A lightbulb came on for me, not just in regard to my own identity, but perhaps also as an explanation of why I found myself much less worried about my son and his development than other parents I had met seemed to feel about their autistic children. Despite my son being mostly nonverbal, I felt I understood him on a deep level and was not all that concerned with whether he would eventually speak or not. I was most concerned with ensuring he was happy. I rejected the traditionally offered therapies, such as Applied Behavioural Analysis (ABA), and simply indulged his interests. I played like he played, tried to see things from his perspective, and figured his childhood would progress pretty much like mine had. I'm happy to say it mostly has, except he is a happier and better version of me, with a secure identity and understanding of his autism that I did not benefit from.

With my own autism diagnosis in hand, I entered into the world of self-advocacy and became involved with many advocacy groups and advocates. I eventually joined the board of Autism Canada. Through these interactions, most of them online on Twitter and Facebook, I was able to connect with thousands of autistic people all over the world.

In my own close entourage, and speaking with autistic people—including, specifically, autistic parents—I've noticed we share many of the same techniques and philosophies. I wanted to test my theories and see if other autistic parents shared not only similar thought patterns, but also similar parenting techniques. I believe our children, both those with autism spectrum disorder (ASD) and those who are neurotypical (NT), benefit from autistic parents' experience in advocacy and how we see the world. When an autistic child has someone in their life who accepts them and understands them, it can only result in good things, namely a secure identity, self-advocacy skills, and healthy self-esteem.

I created an informal survey using SurveyMonkey and shared it in online autistic community groups. I used mostly open-ended questions where participants had to write their responses rather than select from predefined choices, so that parents could freely share what they thought their strengths and challenges were. As I suspected, patterns and repeated themes came out very clearly, and I am sharing those major ones in this book. I want to share the commonalities of how autistic people parent because I believe our methods, and the way we deeply understand the autistic experience, will lead to happier autistic children.

If you aren't sure you understand what your autistic child is going through, or if you want to approach their growth in a way that truly respects their needs, this book is here to guide you in how to parent like an autistic person. This will help you raise happy, well-adjusted autistic kids into amazing autistic adults.

A NOTE ON LANGUAGE: I use the words "Autistic" (sometimes with a capital to denote Autistic culture or people) and "Disabled" as descriptors and as part of my identity. These are used with pride. There is no shame in being Autistic/autistic or Disabled, anymore than there is being a woman, Black, left-handed, or blonde. Just like race and the fact I can't change the colour of my skin, I cannot change my brain. I was born this way. So I do not call myself a person with autism any more than I call myself a person with Blackness. It's not a condition that is separate from me as a person, the way "people-first" language can sometimes imply. I cannot pick up my autism and put it down again when I don't find it convenient. It is with me all the time and it changes the way I see the world. It also creates some challenges for me as we live in a world that is not set up for Autistic or Disabled people. I want to reflect all these truths in my language use.

DON'T SWEAT
THE SMALL STUFF

❯ ❯ ❯ ❯ ❯ ❯ ❯ ❯ ❯ ❯ ❯ ❯ ❯ ❯ ❀❥◗ ❦ ❰ ❰ ❰ ❰ ❰ ❰ ❰ ❰ ❰ ❰ ❰ ❰ ❰

If there's one thing many of us autistic parents share in common, it's the ability to not sweat the small stuff. We really let a lot of behaviours slide, as well as normal childhood clumsiness and mistakes. Perhaps because autistic people often have an overlapping diagnosis of dyspraxia (also known as Developmental Coordination Disorder (DCD), is a common movement disorder affecting fine or gross motor coordination), we are often used to being clumsy ourselves. When our children spill milk, trip over themselves, or just accidentally break things, it really doesn't faze us. We know they can't help it, because we can't either. We know it gets somewhat better with age, but as children, we spent a lot of time choking on air, falling up stairs, and accidentally crushing the butterfly we just caught in our hands.

Even if you have a child who breaks everything they touch the minute they touch it, they have no malicious intent. Please trust us on this one. Your child may be very curious to know what is inside something, but they have no intention to break objects or to make you upset.

One thing I did as a child is tie knots in everything. I took things apart, but I also tied knots in any shoelace or wire I got my hands on. I didn't grow up with tangle toys or spinners, so I guess that's what I did instead. Eventually, after getting in trouble for it enough, I stopped, but it really should not have been a big deal. My parents eventually only bought me shoes with Velcro attachments, but some better, safe alternatives that might have been good replacements for my need to keep my hands busy could have been fidget cubes, tangle bracelets, or even modeling clay. Another thing that could have occupied both my hands and mind would have been a book about how to tie different kinds of knots and some rope for me to practice with.

I've seen parents buy used or broken appliances so that their child could take them apart or fix them. I know more than one autistic person obsessed with vacuums. I know of an autistic man who loves to put together IKEA furniture, so he now makes his living doing that. The point here is that these sorts of hobbies, interests and activities are largely harmless, so it's not worth putting your energy into worrying about them or stopping someone from enjoying them. It's perfectly okay to actively encourage them, even.

Autistic parents are largely okay letting their kids explore the world with all their senses—squishing things, running sand through their hands, licking or sniffing things, staring at lights or running water, not watching where they're going. As a parent, you have to try to stay one step ahead of your kids to keep them safe while they are totally immersed in their world and enjoying the sensations. Join in with them. Try to see things from their perspective and don't sweat it if that's different from yours. If an activity isn't harming your child or others, let it go.

EACH TO THEIR ABILITY,
IN THEIR OWN WAY,
IN THEIR OWN TIME

Sometime before my son turned two, a doctor asked if he was using a fork and spoon to eat. I said no. He told me, "If a child doesn't learn how to use a fork by two years old, they will never learn!"

Oh no! My child was in grave danger of never being able to eat with a fork! Never mind the fact the majority of the world doesn't use forks to eat; most use their hands or chopsticks. But if, let's say, my son simply never learned, would that be the end of the world? If you are ever somewhere without a fork, do you just stare at your plate and wonder how to transport food to your mouth? Would you starve to death because of a lack of forks?

As well, plenty of adults learn to use chopsticks later in life. Surely the same window of opportunity applies to acquiring fork usage skills.

Same thing with potty training. Many parents are particularly concerned their autistic child will never potty train. Guess what? Some don't. They still go on to live amazing lives, even go to university and get jobs. You would be surprised to know the number of both non-disabled and disabled adults who wear diapers or incontinence pads. I know plenty of women who complain they pee a little when they sneeze or laugh, and many a person who "can't trust a fart."

Similar to not sweating the small stuff, it's important to understand that your child will follow their own path and reach so-called developmental milestones in their own time—or not at all. Try to find a way to be okay with that.

Autistic parents know from our own experience that our developmental timeline varies greatly from the neurotypical norm, so we don't parent from the same place of fear that neurotypical (NT) people may. We know our children will get where they need to be in their own time.

That is how you parent like an autistic person. Autistic people are so much more than a checked-off list of developmental milestones or skills. That checklist is not what makes a happy life, and it is not the measure of how intelligent a person is or what they can offer the world.

Let's be real—I have nothing against criminals, but there are plenty of people in prison right now who reached all their developmental milestones perfectly on time. How much value do you really want to place on NT markers of age-based progress?

WHEN CONFLICTING
SENSORY NEEDS COLLIDE

⇒ ⇒ ⇒ ⇒ ⇒ ⇒ ⇒ ⇒ ⇒ ⇒ ⇒ ⇒ ⇒ ⇒ ⇒ ⇐ ⇐ ⇐ ⇐ ⇐ ⇐ ⇐ ⇐ ⇐ ⇐ ⇐ ⇐

In a mixed autistic-NT household, you will need to try and balance mixed accommodation needs. I won't sugar-coat it: sometimes this is very challenging. Even in majority-autistic households, trying to address the needs of those who are sensory-avoidant (those whose sensory systems do not favour a lot of external stimulus, and will avoid loud or unexpected noises, touching, tickles, certain fabrics) with sensory-seekers (those craving and needing a lot of sensory feedback or stimulation, favouring touch, intense body sensations, spicy foods, loud or constant noise) will call for creativity.

You may have an extrovert in your family who loves to go out and enjoys being with large groups of people, and you may have a homebody who wants to stay in and be in silence. For autistic parents, our sensitive sensory systems mean we need to make accommodations for both ourselves and our children when we are parenting. The autistic parents I surveyed agreed that this is by far the most challenging aspect of parenting.

Your child may engage in random bouts of echolalic behaviours (repeating sounds) that just become annoying, whether you are autistic or not. My son hums, jumps and flaps. It can be tiring to hear near-constant humming. It only stops when he is asleep, and we know the minute he is awake. At the same time, when I hear it, I know he's happy. When he's away at respite for the day, I miss the sound. I wish I had an amazing solution so I could tell you exactly what to do, but I don't.

In my case, I put a positive spin on my son's stim (repeated behaviours). He is happy when he is stimming, so I try to feel his joy and just content myself with the fact he feels safe doing it around me, my partner, and our other son. On that note, society often looks down on what they see as "weird behaviours" like flapping, humming, rocking, or other common autistic behaviours, and educational and therapeutic settings often seek to stop children from stimming. I feel stimming is natural and enjoyable and should not be stopped. An autistic person may try to repress themselves in order to fit in, which usually leads to feelings of shame. I would much rather our son feel safe to be who he is. Home should be a place of sanctuary from outside judgement.

I have spoken to many autistic parents who are, for example, sensory-avoidant but have sensory-seeking children. Autistic parents may stretch out of their comfort zone, sensory-wise, in order to give their child what they need. Whether you're autistic or not, I am not advocating for total self-sacrifice in your parenting, but understand there may be aspects of parenting that push you out of your comfort zone, at least from time to time.

As parents, we all have to manage our own needs and sensory regulation every day by taking time for ourselves and regulating ourselves first. All parents must prioritize self-care, but this is especially important for families that have family members who need extra caregiving. Trouble dealing with noise is probably the number-one complaint I hear from autistic parents. When my first son was born, being unpredictably woken up at night to his cries was at first so disturbing to me that I felt physically ill. Some parents may wear earplugs or ear defenders (noise-canceling headphones) in their homes.

Learning to emotionally regulate yourself first should be a priority. This is a skill that can be learned at any stage of life, but many of us did not adequately learn it as children. If you find your own patience lacking, you may need to seek out a trained psychotherapist to help you learn these skills or add some new coping tools. Once you gain these skills, you can help your child learn to as well. The point here is that when it comes to accommodation, the onus is on the parent and should not be placed on the child.

An autistic parent generally knows they can't change their sensory-seeking child into a sensory-avoidant one for the parent's convenience. You must come up with creative ways to parent the child you have without trying to change them.

YES, WE REALLY
ARE THAT UNAWARE

How could you?
Why would you?
Did he really just do that?
Did she say that?
I know she knows better!

Autistic people have heard these things more times than we'd ever want to admit. Especially given that we may succeed quite well at school or in the workforce, it can be hard to fathom how we could possibly be so unaware or "unintelligent" in other areas of our lives. But the concept of "he should know by now not to say or do that" unfortunately doesn't apply to many autistic adults.

Because autism is a developmental disorder, an autistic person's learning and skills development are often uneven, and our lack of social awareness means we miss many of the subtle cues or hints neurotypical people give out and perceive almost subconsciously. Unless we are explicitly shown what to do or say, or what something means, we honestly don't know.

With this in mind, it is important to use plain language when teaching your autistic child. Even if you have a child who is highly intelligent and knows all the capital cities of all the countries in the world, you may have to show them how to open a door for someone else, and practice doing so, and explain why holding a door open for someone is a nice gesture, all in painstaking detail.

I truly believe that when someone can do better, they do. When your child makes a social gaffe, says something too blunt, or pulls down their pants at the dinner table, you have to give them the benefit of the doubt. They are not trying to be difficult. They are not trying to embarrass you or anyone else. They are not doing it for attention (though there should be nothing wrong with that either), and they certainly do not know better.

Autistic people are extremely sensitive and we are people-pleasers. We want to get it right. We beat ourselves up horribly when we make a mistake and we want to fix it. We don't forget our mistakes, and they sometimes replay in our heads for years.

Autistic children desperately want to make their parents proud. Don't be the source of shame or the face of disappointment burned into their memories.

DON'T JUDGE A BOOK
BY ITS COVER

A utistic people in general are some of the most non-judgemental people you'll ever meet. Not much fazes us, and perhaps because of our tendency to not worry about gender norms or sexual orientation, we are commonly very open to the full spectrum of sexuality and gender. A high number of autistic people express gender variance themselves or may be transgender. Be prepared for your autistic child to possibly not be cisgender (as in, to identify with their sex at birth) or straight.

As well, we make friends with people in different age groups and of different races and classes without putting much thought into it. Your autistic child, unless they receive messages from you or outside society, will likely grow up not judging people for their appearance or differences. As adults, we tend to find acceptance in other "outsiders" and be friends with a wide variety of people, within a large age range. By extension, as parents, we tend to automatically accept our children for who they are, exactly as they are.

If you want to parent like an autistic person, you need to keep your mind open and accept the person your child is growing into. It will also help if you can give them the language they need to describe their feelings and the great variety of people they will meet in life. Speak openly with them about gender identity, sexuality, different kinds of families, and different religions and races.

One common theme that came up in my survey of autistic parents is they all report very close relationships with their children and say they are able to speak openly about any issue. Our children know they can come to us and speak about anything and not be judged. Our natural tendency towards honesty and straightforwardness also means that not much gets sugar-coated. We tend to allow our children a lot more bodily autonomy and agency (within age-appropriate limits) and involve them in any discussions that will affect them and their future. For instance, I have explained all my son's psychological evaluations and reports to him in plain language so he can understand his diagnosis, and he is involved in his Individualized Education Plan (IEP) meetings.

More so than NT parents, autistic parents give their children a lot of freedom and control, and this fosters a relationship of trust, respect, and openness. As an NT parent, taking a similar approach will help you cultivate a happy relationship with your child.

WE ARE
CREATURES OF HABIT

Routine is important for most autistic people. Autistic children are often seen as very rigid and can have a meltdown when faced with any change to their routine. These reactions can be very challenging for parents, and I've heard some NT parents say they feel like they are at the mercy of their child. To some extent, this is absolutely true, but it's also temporary. I promise your child will become less rigid with time.

Autistic or not, I think we can appreciate that all people are really creatures of habit. Without knowing you, I can almost guarantee you prefer to buy the same brand of coffee or toothpaste, take the same route to work each day, go to the same restaurants over and over, and order the exact same meal as always. Writing this now, seven months into the 2020 global coronavirus pandemic, I have watched as people suddenly struggled to cope the moment their daily routine was disrupted, and they could not go to work or shop as they usually did. Overnight, people became listless and lost, not showering or changing their clothes, staying in comfy jogging pants and pyjamas. When the world is chaotic, we cling to and depend on our routines to ground us and make us feel safe.

Autistic people's brains lack the sensory filters NTs have. We also lack the ability to make good predictions of other people's actions or behaviours. For an autistic child (and many adults), the world is always chaotic. If you struggled during the beginning of the pandemic with the sudden loss of your routine, it gave you just a small taste of what autistic people go through every single day.

The way to help autistic people feel safe in becoming less rigid is to actually not try to force them not to be. If you stick to the routine and create a safe environment for them, they will start to take a few risks and experiment with small changes to their routine, for instance by trying a taste of a different food. I can imagine many NT parents shaking their heads in disbelief at this suggestion, but trust me on this one. Keep familiar foods and routines the same—without judgement, without complaint, without coercion, without sighing, without yelling—and one day your child will surprise you.

As a child, I did everything on my own time when I was good and ready. I didn't really branch out into trying new foods until I met my husband when I was 19 years old. He never judged me, he just regularly offered me a bite of whatever he was eating. He didn't say, "Oh my gosh, you've never tried this before?" or "You don't like it? What's wrong with you?" No pressure; he just offered me a chance to try and that was it. Safe and simple. It worked for me, and the same approach has worked on my son. Reduce outside pressures or demands, and the child will come out of their protective shell.

Autistic parents thrive on routine. We need it for ourselves—to stay present, focused and organized—and we run our households with the same military precision. All children thrive on routine and visual reminders, but neurodivergent children especially so. Predictability lowers anxiety levels, which results in fewer meltdowns or "problem behaviours."

Create that safe environment for your child for the time they need it and I promise you will see them blossom. Everyone changes over time, autistic kids included, and it's not healthy to try to force them to change faster by using shame or coercion, or by putting them into anxiety-producing situations. I do not advocate for "exposure therapy" (putting people in stressful situations for progressively longer periods to desensitize them) and I do not advocate any feeding therapy that forces a person to eat bites of food they do not like. When a child knows you will validate and accept their feelings and experiences of the world, and also protect them from what scares them, they are more likely to become brave enough to test the waters and see for themselves that the world is not that scary.

WE TRULY DON'T CARE WHAT YOU THINK

Maybe because we don't pick up on social cues as well or as easily as NT people, or at all, we are not only less likely to conform or give into peer pressure, but we also truly don't care what others think about us. So when an autistic parent is out in public with their autistic child who is humming and flapping, and people are staring, we just keep going about our business without bother. In my case, if I notice someone staring at my son while he is stimming, I actually join in with him. So if one person stimming was bothering you, well, now it's doubled. Enjoy!

When our children have a meltdown in public, our full attention goes to taking care of our child. We ignore the stares, the dirty looks, and the ignorant comments. Or again, not being concerned with conformity and decorum means we might very quickly and bluntly tell people where to go while we focus on keeping our child safe.

As a parent, your priority is to help your child. So if there's only one skill you develop while trying to parent like an autistic, make it the ability to let the negative stuff from outsiders who don't know better slide off your back. Keep marching your family to the beat of your own drum. Don't waste a moment of energy on strangers. Just focus on your child. At the end of the day, you see them smile or you get that special moment of recognition that only you understand, and it's all worth it, isn't it?

BEHAVIOUR IS COMMUNICATION

"Behaviour is communication" is a phrase that has been slowly coming into use in therapeutic and educational settings. The premise is that it's important to understand why someone is doing something, especially when they cannot express their reasons in words.

We understand now that sometimes, aggression or repetitive behaviours actually stem from the pain an individual feels, if they lack the means to explain that pain. While autistic people often don't have adequate communication methods (spoken language, signed language or augmented communication), even people who have methods of communication may act out their feelings instead. This happens simply because a person's interoception (meaning their ability to clearly sense what's going on inside their body) is not fully developed, or their sensory system is in a state of dysregulation.

For example, for autistic people, it can be hard to localize pain in our bodies. We may know our stomach hurts, but not be able to tell you exactly where. I didn't actually have the ability to feel hunger pangs until I was 13, and when I did, it was quite a surprise for me because I didn't initially know what they were. I didn't even realize I was having migraines until adulthood, despite having suffered from them for many years. Sometimes, autistic people sense pain, but then sort of ignore it and keep on going with things.

I took these lessons into my parenting. Before my son could speak, I became a "Dr. Mom" and bought a stethoscope (to listen to heartbeat and breathing), otoscope (to look into ears, nose and throat), glucose meter (to measure blood sugar levels), and oximeter (to measure blood oxygen levels). I learned that when my son starts a fever, he becomes very social, touchy, and chatty—all very uncharacteristic of him. When he feels nauseated, he asks me to sit next to him. When he goes completely quiet and starts to hide from me, I know something hurts. Sometimes it's just a tiny cut on his finger. In short, parents of autistic children need to be tuned in to our children and keep watch for when something seems off or out of character.

If your child is acting differently, check for signs of discomfort. At bath time, check their body for cuts or bruises. Look for any tiny strings or hairs that may have gotten caught around a toe or finger, or embedded in skin. I really advise doing this daily— especially if your child does not have reliable verbal communication patterns, but even if they do. This kind of checking is especially important if they attend a school or day centre and you don't know what happens to them during the day. You can also try using pictograms or have them draw a picture to try to communicate with them.

Some autistic people will bang their head when they have a headache, or grind their teeth when they have tooth or mouth pain. What might look like a stim is actually an expression of pain. Some therapists will instead suggest trying to get the child to stop stimming, and not realize that if they solved the underlying pain issue, the behaviour would go away.

The main takeaway I'm suggesting here is that every behaviour an autistic person engages in has a good reason. We don't act out due to maliciousness—that is not generally in our character and is not one of the diagnostic traits of autism. We are more prone to self-injurious behaviours (head banging, biting ourselves) out of frustration for not being able to express our needs.

Trust that if your child is exhibiting troubling behaviours, they are trying to communicate something, and punishment is not warranted. Also, no amount of therapy is likely to stop the behaviour until the root cause is found—but some approaches may force them to suppress their behaviour, thus depriving you of the information you need to keep your child healthy and safe.

CONCLUSION

If you're a neurotypical parent who has taken the time to read this, and you're open to learning from autistic adults, you are already showing that you want to do the best for your child. That's amazing! Take a moment to pat yourself on the back. Many of us autistic adults wish we had been parented this way, with love and acceptance. On behalf of autistic adults everywhere, I thank you for what you are doing and wish you and your family happiness and health.

ABOUT THE AUTHOR

K. Bron Johnson is an Autistic and Hard of Hearing self-advocate born, raised and living in Montreal, Canada. She is the founder of Completely Inclusive, a social enterprise consultancy focused on Inclusion and Accessibility in the workplace. She and her partner are raising two neurodivergent boys. This book, and all her work, is dedicated to helping create a truly inclusive society, where everyone can feel free to be their authentic selves and contribute to the best of their ability.